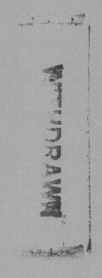

RIVERS THROUGH TIME

Settlements of the
MISSISSIPPI
River

Rob Bowden

Heinemann Library
Chicago, Illinois

© 2005 Heinemann Library
a division of Reed Elsevier Inc.
Chicago, Illinois

Customer Service   888–454–2279

Visit our website at www.heinemannlibrary.com

Photo research by Ruth Blair and Ginny Stroud-Lewis
Designed by Richard Parker and Tinstar Design Ltd (www.tinstar.co.uk)
Printed in China by WKT Company Limited

09 08 07 06 05
10 9 8 7 6 5 4 3 2 1

Library of Congress Cataloging-in-Publication Data
Bowden, Rob.
   Settlements of the Mississippi River / Rob Bowden.
      p. cm. -- (Rivers through time)
   Includes bibliographical references and index.
   ISBN 1-4034-5719-0 -- ISBN 1-4034-5724-7 (pbk.)
1. Mississippi River--History--Juvenile literature. 2. Mississippi River Valley--History--Juvenile literature. 3. Mississippi River Valley--History, Local--Juvenile literature. 4. Cities and towns--Mississippi River Valley--History--Juvenile literature. 5. Land settlement--Mississippi River Valley--History--Juvenile literature. I. Title. II. Series.
   F351.B68 2004
   977--dc22
                          2004002423

Acknowledgments
The publishers would like to thank the following for permission to reproduce photographs:
Alamy p. 14; Corbis pp. 12, 18, 19, 26; Corbis pp. 21, 27, 28, 31, 32 (Bettman), 33 (Kevin Fleming), 20 (the Mariners Museum), 34 (Buddy Mays), 40 (Minnesota Historical Society), 39 (Bill Ross); Eye Ubiquitous pp. 5, 8, 17; Hutchison p. 22; Lonely Planet p. 13; Minnesota Historical Society p. 37; National Park Services p. 11; North Winds Picture Archive pp. 4, 9; Pictures colour library pp. 15, 23, 29, 42

Cover photograph reproduced with permission of Lonely Planet Images.

Illustrator: Stephen Sweet (pp. 7, 10, 16, 24, 30, 36) Jeff Edwards (pp. 25, 34, 38, 40, 42)

Contents

Words in bold, **like this**, are explained in the Glossary.

Introducing the Mississippi River

The mighty Mississippi

The Mississippi River carries more water than any other river in North America. It stretches from north to south, right across the United States, for a total distance of 2,350 miles (3,780 kilometers). The Mississippi and its major **tributary,** the Missouri River, combine to form the Mississippi–Missouri river system. This river system stretches 3,710 miles (5,970 kilometers) and is the fourth longest in the world. The Mississippi River is one of the United State's main geographical features and has also played a central role in the country's history.

This hut is a replica of the type of river dwellings that were built on the Mississippi by Native Americans.

River glossary

Confluence – *the point where two rivers join.*

Delta – *where the river joins the sea.*

Mouth – *the ending point of a river.*

Reaches – *used to describe sections of the river (upper, middle, and lower reaches).*

River course – *the path followed by a river from source to mouth.*

Source – *the starting point of a river.*

Tributary – *a river or stream that joins another (usually bigger) river.*

Archaeological evidence shows that Native Americans lived alongside the Mississippi as far back as 12,000 years ago. All that remains of these ancient **settlements** are earthen mounds. These have given the name *the mound builders* to these Native Americans. Some mounds were bases for important buildings, such as chiefs' houses or **shrines.** Others were burial mounds.

Settlers would have been attracted to the river for similar reasons. With no roads or railroads, the river was the quickest way to travel and the best way to carry **trade** goods between settlements. The Mississippi also provided fish, and its fertile **floodplains** were good for farming.

Today, the Mississippi is one of the busiest rivers in the world and one of the United State's major transportation routes. It also provides water to some of the country's best farmland and to such big cities as Minneapolis and St. Louis. The Mississippi River has also become a center of American **culture**. It was the source for blues music and rock and roll from Memphis and jazz music and the world-famous **Mardi Gras** carnival in New Orleans.

Tow barges transport cargo along the Mississippi River – one of the world's busiest waterways.

The Mississippi from source to mouth

The source of the Mississippi is in Minnesota close to the Canadian border. The river emerges from Lake Itasca at a relatively low **altitude** of just 1,475 feet (450 meters). Lake Itasca is a clear, shallow lake surrounded by pine forests. It was named Itasca by the explorer Henry Rowe Schoolcraft in 1832. The name comes from the Latin words *veritas caput*, which mean "true head." It refers to the source, or head, of the river. The waters leave Lake Itasca over a line of underwater boulders. Many tourists visit this place to walk across the waters of the Mississippi as it begins its journey south to the Gulf of Mexico.

In its upper **reaches,** the Mississippi flows through a marshy area of many small lakes and streams. There are few settlements here, but the region is a popular place for walking, fishing, and camping. There are also reservations for Native American groups as the Ojibwe, who still live near the source of the Mississippi. In the twin cities of Minneapolis and St. Paul, the Mississippi flows over St. Anthony's Falls. This is the only set of waterfalls on the entire river. Downstream, the Mississippi widens and becomes **navigable.** Between here and St. Louis (a distance of about 670 miles or 1,080 kilometers) the river is joined by most of its major tributaries, which include the Minnesota, Wisconsin, Illinois, and Missouri rivers.

The middle reaches of the Mississippi stretch for around 200 miles (330 kilometers) between St. Louis and the river's **confluence** with the Ohio River at Cairo, Illinois. It flows much faster in this section and becomes murky brown in color after it joins the Missouri River just north of St. Louis. The color is caused by large quantities of **silt** that are carried by the Missouri. They give the Missouri its other name, "the big muddy." After the confluence with the Ohio River, the Mississippi slows and widens as it enters its long, lower reaches. The river is now 1.5 miles (2.5 kilometers) wide in places. It begins to **meander** wildly from side to side, sometimes almost going back on itself. The Mississippi is joined by many more tributaries before it finally enters the swamps and **bayous** near New Orleans. This is the Mississippi **delta,** a giant wetland where the river slows and deposits its silt before finally joining the Gulf of Mexico.

UNITED STATES OF AMERICA

CANADA

MINNESOTA
Lake Itasca

Minneapolis
St. Paul
Mississippi River
WISCONSIN
Madison

Rocky Mountains

New York

IOWA
Missouri River
Des Moines
Illinois River
ILLINOIS
Indianapolis
INDIANA
OHIO
Springfield
WEST VIRGINIA
Ohio River

Jefferson City
St. Louis
MISSOURI
KENTUCKY

Appalachian Mountains

KEY
- Case study location
- State capital
- River
- National border
- State border

Mississippi River
Nashville
ARKANSAS
TENNESSEE
Arkansas River
Memphis
Little Rock

N
E
S

| 0 | Miles | 300 |
| 0 | Kilometers | 500 |

MISSISSIPPI

ALABAMA

ATLANTIC OCEAN

LOUISIANA
Jackson

MEXICO

Baton Rouge
New Orleans
Mississippi Delta
FLORIDA

GULF OF MEXICO

7

Settlements of the Mississippi

The Mississippi River does not run through any mountains or high ground, so people have been able to settle along almost its entire length. Many of these settlements are just small farming communities. People have settled here to take advantage of the fertile floodplains of the Mississippi. These provide some of the best farmland in the United States and are one of the most heavily farmed areas in the world. The major crops include corn, cotton, and sugar. The Mississippi is central to the farming industry because it provides water for **irrigation**. More importantly, it is a transportation route for taking produce to other parts of the country or the world. In 2003, almost half of the U.S. grain exports were transported down the Mississippi.

What's in a name?
The name Mississippi originates with the Dakota people, who once lived in the area north of St. Louis. They referred to the river as the Father of Waters. In their language this was said as Misi, *meaning big, and* Sipi, *meaning water.*

The land surrounding the Mississippi is some of the most fertile American farmland.

Paddle-wheel steamboats brought big changes to the Mississippi and its settlements.

The combination of farming, river transportation, and trade led to the development of several settlements into larger towns and cities. These places are often located at important points on the river. Minneapolis and St. Louis, for example, are at places where the Mississippi is joined by another river. Other settlements became important stopping places for the **steamboats** that dramatically changed transportation on the Mississippi in the 1800s. For example, Memphis became a trading point between the important market town of St. Louis and the growing ports of Baton Rouge and New Orleans, Louisiana.

In this book, we will explore some of the best-known settlements of the Mississippi River. We will follow a passage through time, starting with Baton Rouge and ending in Minneapolis, which today is the biggest settlement on the Mississippi. We will look at why each settlement was founded where it was, and at how it changed over time. What are the settlements like today and how might they change in the future? Most importantly, we will discover how the settlements are connected to the Mississippi and to the lives of the people living there. This will show us how the importance of the Mississippi and the surrounding area has changed over time.

9

Baton Rouge: Ancient Mounds and Oil

The red stick

The first European to discover the Mississippi River was the Spanish explorer and conquistador Hernando de Soto. De Soto's expedition to explore what is now the southern United States began in 1538. In 1541, he found the Mississippi. However, sick with fever, de Soto died on its banks in early 1542. Although de Soto discovered the Mississippi for the Spanish, French explorers founded many of the first **settlements** along the river.

In 1699, Pierre Le Moyne d'Iberville, a French-Canadian naval captain, sailed up the Mississippi to protect the **territory of Louisiana,** which was controlled by the French. D'Iberville noticed a red stick standing some 30 feet (9 meters) high on a hill to one side of the river. The stick had fish heads and bear bones attached to it, and looked as though it had been part of a Native American ceremony. It is now thought that the post was a boundary marker between the Houma and the Bayougoula Indians. D'Iberville named the location after this marker, which in French was *baton* (which means "stick") *rouge* (which means "red").

Four nations fought over Baton Rouge because of its location on the Mississippi.

The red stick was a useful marker of high ground first found by sailing upstream from the coast. The location made it an obvious place to build a settlement. The high ground provided protection from flooding and a good position for defending any form of attack. In spite of these obvious advantages, early French settlements were temporary. However, they did build a fort there in 1719. Baton Rouge's early

ARKANSAS

MISSISSIPPI

LOUISIANA

Jackson

TEXAS

ALABA

Baton Rouge

New Orleans

Mississippi L

GULF OF MEXICO

Mound builders

A series of mounds located in Baton Rouge provide evidence of early Native American settlements along the Mississippi. The mounds are believed to date back around 5,000 years. The mounds might have been burial mounds or platforms for ceremonies. They might have been places where people met to go hunting and gathering. Whatever their true purpose, they serve as a reminder to the people of Baton Rouge of their town's Native American origins.

The Native American Mound of Bear Creek in the state of Mississippi.

development was dominated by military struggles for the Mississippi. The French, Spanish, British, and Americans all wanted to gain control of the river and its valuable traffic. Between 1763 and 1810, Baton Rouge changed five times. It finally became part of the United States in 1810. In that year, local Americans rebelled against the Spanish rulers and claimed Baton Rouge for the West Florida Republic. Three months later the Republic became part of the United States.

Open for business

Baton Rouge began to grow bigger and more prosperous. This is because paddle-wheel **steamboats** arrived to bring trade in animal skins or timber, and eventually in farm produce. The first steamboat to pull into Baton Rouge, the *New Orleans*, arrived in 1812. Within just 10 years, traffic on the river increased sharply. In 1822, 174 **barges** and 441 **flatboats** visited Baton Rouge. The trade attracted many businesses to Baton Rouge, and they all depended on the river.

11

Changing times

Baton Rouge's **economy** got a boost when the government decided to build an army post in the town. The Pentagon Barracks were built in 1819 to defend the Mississippi River from future attacks. The soldiers stationed there increased the demand for local goods and services. In 1820, a ferry service across the Mississippi began, and this allowed trade across the river. The town developed rapidly. By 1840, the population of Baton Rouge had grown to 2,269. The riverfront was still the center of activity and the **wharves** bustled with river traffic, trading cotton, sugar, and at that time, slaves, too. By 1860, the town's population had doubled to 5,428. It now had coffee houses, a foundry, and a prison. Most importantly, though, Baton Rouge had become the state capital of Louisiana. It still serves that role today.

In 1862, Baton Rouge was badly damaged during the **Civil War** because it was the scene of several small fights between the Union and Confederate forces. Union forces made the first move when they sailed their gunboats up the Mississippi from New Orleans. At first they took the town with little struggle, but on August 5, 1862, Confederate forces launched an attack to recapture the town. This became known

Slavery

One of the more troubling episodes in the history of the Mississippi is the role it played in slavery. Thousands of slaves, most of them from Africa, were traded up and down the river. In 1860, slaves made up around a quarter of the population of Baton Rouge. Disagreement over whether it was right to keep slaves was one of the major causes of the Civil War (1861 to 1865). The Confederates supported slavery; the Union wanted it abolished. When the Union forces claimed Baton Rouge in 1862, many freed slaves flocked to the city, and by 1865 African Americans made up the majority of the population. They remained the majority until as recently as 1920.

A photo of the Pentagon Barracks during the Civil War. The Barracks still stand on the riverfront today, and are some of the oldest surviving buildings in the town.

as the Battle of Baton Rouge. The Confederate forces drove the Union forces back as far as the river, where the Union naval fleet was moored. This river power put the Union forces in a better position than the that of the Confederates. The Union's powerful gunboats forced the Confederates to abandon Baton Rouge and to get out of the boats' target range. Within a few hours the Union won the battle, but the victory was costly. About a third of the town had been destroyed.

Baton Rouge did not begin to recover until the end of the Civil War. The river was key in this recovery, and steamer traffic was the main business of the town for many years. As the town was rebuilt, several new industries developed. These included a **lumber** company, a brick-making factory, and a **mill** for processing cottonseed into oil. In 1883, the railroad arrived in Baton Rouge. Because of this, ports and industries gradually expanded along the Mississippi waterfront.

Oil wealth

The most striking growth of Baton Rouge came during the early 1900s. In 1909, Standard Oil chose Baton Rouge as the location for a new oil refinery. Standard Oil was one of the United States' biggest oil companies. Baton Rouge was close to the oilfields of Texas, Louisiana, and Oklahoma, and the Mississippi River was deep enough at the town to receive large

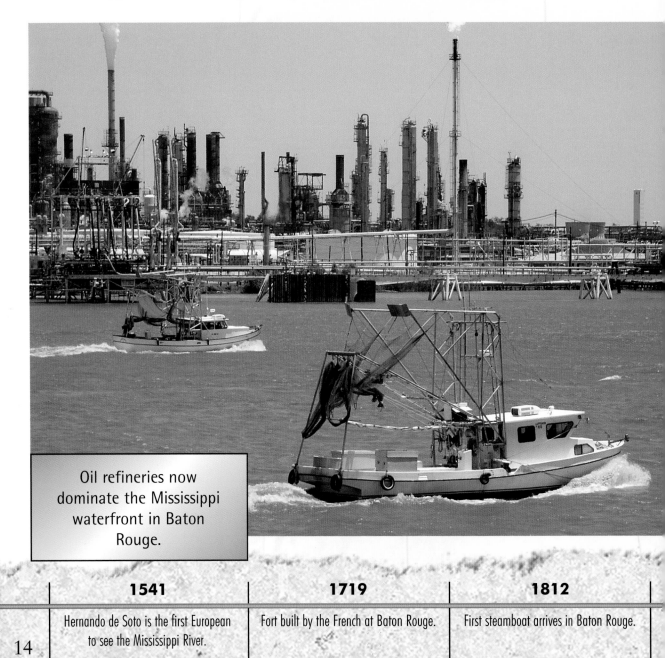

Oil refineries now dominate the Mississippi waterfront in Baton Rouge.

1541	1719	1812
Hernando de Soto is the first European to see the Mississippi River.	Fort built by the French at Baton Rouge.	First steamboat arrives in Baton Rouge.

ocean-going oil tankers. Standard Oil built their own docks on the Mississippi River in order to handle the special oil freight. Other industries followed Standard Oil, so in the 1920s the docks were upgraded to meet their needs. Baton Rouge now has special dock facilities for handling general cargo and such goods as grain, **molasses**, and timber.

Baton Rouge's oil industry played a particularly important role during World War II (1939 to 1945). The town's refineries provided around three-quarters of the country's aviation fuel, and supplied hundreds of American aircraft involved in the war. With so much work available in the town during the 1940s, Baton Rouge's population more than trebled from around 35,000 to 125,000.

Baton Rouge remains one of the most important U.S. ports today, and oil continues to be its major industry. The Mississippi is still the focus of its industry and economy. Oil, timber, and agricultural goods are the main **products** passing through the port today. During the 1980s, Baton Rouge began to take advantage of tourist interest in the history of the city and the river. Today, visitors can take a cruise in a replica Mississippi steamer or tour one of the old plantation homes that once thrived in the area.

The jobs created by tourism and government business helped Baton Rouge's population continue growing throughout the second half of the 1900s. Louisiana State University is also a major employer. Its staff and students number 34,000 in total and help support many local businesses. By the year 2000, the population of the **metropolitan** area had reached almost 603,000.

1819	1862	1883	1909
Pentagon Barracks are built at Baton Rouge.	Union forces claim Baton Rouge, and slaves are freed.	Railroad arrives in Baton Rouge.	Standard Oil build a new refinery in Baton Rouge.

New Orleans: The Crescent City

City in a swamp

The city of New Orleans has an unusual location in the middle of the Mississippi **delta,** which is a vast marshy swamp. The delta is a hot and wet environment that has frequent hurricanes and floods and is infested with mosquitoes. Also, very little land lies above the level of the river. The dry land that exists is not rock, but mud that was deposited by the river over thousands of years. This hardly sounds like a good location for a **settlement.**

New Orleans became a settlement because it lies at the mouth of the mighty Mississippi River. At the time

FACT

New Orleans has suffered damage from hurricanes. In 1794, much of the city was destroyed by a series of three hurricanes.

New Orleans' position at the mouth of the Mississippi made it a very desirable site for early settlers, despite its very hot and wet climate.

New Orleans is surrounded by the waters of the Mississippi delta. The crescent that gives the city its nickname is clearly visible.

the river was the only trade route into the heart of North America. Whoever controlled this area controlled the valuable river trade between the U.S. interior and the rest of the world. The site of New Orleans was first spotted by French explorers as early as 1682, but there are no signs that the area was settled until 1718. That was when Jean-Baptiste le Moyne de Bienville, a governor of French Louisiana, laid out the early section of the city on a sharp bend in the Mississippi. New Orleans gets its nickname, "the Crescent City," from the crescent shape of this sharp bend.

The first settlers in New Orleans were a mix of passing Mississippi traders, European settlers, and slaves of mostly African origin. A census in 1721 stated that there were 470 people living in New Orleans. During the next year, New Orleans was declared the capital of the French **territory of Louisiana.** The French were confident about the settlement. However, New Orleans grew slowly at first. There were few valuable trading goods in the local area. European merchants did not want to visit unless they could fill their ships' holds with worthwhile cargoes for the journey home. The French tried to encourage investment in New Orleans. However, this failed, causing problems in France as well as in New Orleans. By the middle of the 1700s, New Orleans had become a financial burden. In 1763, France gave New Orleans and Louisiana west of the Mississippi to the Spanish. The rest of Louisiana went to the British, who defeated France in the Seven Years War (1756 to 1763).

The city awakens

Under Spanish control, New Orleans began to prosper. It attracted new settlers, and by the turn of the century the population of New Orleans had grown to around 8,000 people. The city's growth was due to its location at the mouth of the Mississippi. By 1800, New Orleans had become an important storage and shipping center. It handled local sugar and rice, as well as cotton, wheat, timber, and other goods from farther upstream. In New Orleans, **commodities** were loaded onto larger ocean-going ships heading for Europe or the east coast of the newly formed United States. Manufactured goods also came through New Orleans from Europe, making their way up the Mississippi to Baton Rouge and St. Louis.

In 1800, New Orleans came back under French control, but only for a short time. In 1803 it was sold, with the rest of Louisiana, to the United States in a deal known as the **Louisiana Purchase.**

In 1815, U.S. forces successfully fought off the British, who were trying to take control of New Orleans.

Mississippi flatboats

*Mississippi **flatboats** were a common sight in the early days of New Orleans. These large wooden rafts were made upstream of New Orleans, loaded with grain from Missouri or Illinois, and then guided downstream by teams of workers with long poles. Along the way, they faced many hazards, incuding floods, alligators, and even pirates who tried to steal their cargo. When the flatboat crew reached New Orleans, the workers would sell their cargo to the traders in the city. The workers even sold the wood that their rafts were made of because the river current was too powerful to make the return journey. Instead, the flatboat crew would begin the long walk home, a journey that could take up to three months.*

Soon after the Americans gained New Orleans, they had to defend it from a British naval attack. In 1812 the United States declared war on Great Britain over the control of highly valuable shipping routes across the Atlantic. New Orleans was an important target for the British armed forces because whoever ruled New Orleans would have control of the Mississippi and its river trade. When the British attacked in January 1815, U.S. forces and local volunteers were ready for them. They launched a barrage of artillery and musket fire, killing the British commander and forcing the British to retreat. New Orleans was saved for the Americans. The Battle of New Orleans need never have happened, however, for just a few days earlier the British and Americans had signed a peace agreement in Belgium.

The boom years

The steamboat, a new and efficient form of transportation, was introduced in 1812. Soon, New Orleans became a wealthy town. Improvements in cotton farming had led to an expansion of cotton plantations along the Mississippi. Millions of bales of cotton began to be sent by steamboat to New Orleans. From there, the bales were reloaded onto ocean-going ships for the journey to the **textile mills** of Great Britain.

The boom in river transportation led to a huge demand for workers. Thousands of people were needed to load and unload the river boats and work in the warehouses. Jobs were also

FACT

By 1840, New Orleans was the fourth most important port in the whole world!

Mississippi steamboats line the waterfront in New Orleans. The steamboat brought great wealth to the city.

created to provide housing, food, clothing, and even entertainment for the river workers and their families. Many people who came to work in the warehouses were **immigrants** from Ireland, Germany, Great Britain, Spain, and Italy, as well as from other parts of the United States. Thousands of slaves were brought in to meet the demand for workers. The city's population grew from 8,000 in 1803 to almost 170,000 by 1860.

Many new neighborhoods were built to house the growing population. These were known as "'faubourgs'" (suburbs) in New Orleans. Faubourg Sainte Marie developed as a mainly American neighborhood, while Faubourg Tremé was a neighborhood in which freed African slaves lived. One of New Orleans' biggest problems was frequent flooding caused by the Mississippi or heavy rains, which are common in the city. Artificial embankments called *levees* were built along the banks of the Mississippi to prevent the river from flooding onto the settlements below them. Levees did not always work, however; New Orleans has flooded several times when the levees failed to hold back the Mississippi. Much of New Orleans still lies below the level of the Mississippi and is protected by levees.

> This shows aftermath of serious flooding along the Mississippi.

Changing fortunes

After the **Civil War** (1861 to 1865), New Orleans continued to grow, but it faced many problems. The Civil War hurt cotton production, and factories in Great Britain began buying their cotton from other places. Goods that had once been carried down the Mississippi to New Orleans were soon taken directly by railroad to east coast cities and ports, such as New York. In the early 1900s, New Orleans began to prosper again when the development of **towboats** and river **barges** made river transportation more popular. One towboat could tow fifteen barges, and each barge could carry as much cargo as fifteen rail cars. This made Mississippi towboats the most efficient way to transport bulky cargoes like **petroleum,** coal, steel, sand, grain, and **minerals.** From the 1950s on, the oil industry also brought a boost to New Orleans. **Petrochemical** plants and refineries were

This causeway over Lake Pontchartrain provides a vital road link for New Orleans. It is one of the longest causeways in the world.

1682

French explorers discover the site that becomes New Orleans.

1718

Jean-Baptiste le Moyne de Bienville plans New Orleans.

traditions of the African Americans who lived in New Orleans. The world-famous jazz musician Louis Armstrong was born in New Orleans in 1901. He spent his early career playing the cornet in the dance bands of Mississippi River boats.

Creole and Cajun food also developed in New Orleans. They developed over the years from a mix of cooking traditions that include Native American, French, Spanish, and African recipes. The most famous dishes are gumbo and jambalaya.

This combination of history, music, and food has turned New Orleans into a major tourist destination. The Mississippi River is important for this growing industry. Replica steamboats take passengers on cruises up the Mississippi to trace the path of explorers who ventured upriver some 300 years ago to found New Orleans. As it did then, the river remains the reason for the very existence of New Orleans, a true city of the Mississippi.

established along the Mississippi north of New Orleans. The city became a center for exploring oil reserves beneath the Mississippi delta.

Culture and tourism

New Orleans is among the most historically important cities in the United States. The city has created its own culture, and it is famous as the birthplace of jazz music in the early 1900s. Jazz came from the musical

1763	1803	1900s
France gives New Orleans to the Spanish.	New Orleans is bought by the United States in the Louisiana Purchase.	Jazz music begins to develop in New Orleans.

St. Louis: The Gateway City

A trade post

St. Louis is located roughly halfway down the Mississippi in the state of Missouri. In 1763, two French men, Pierre Laclede and his stepson Auguste Chouteau, traveled up the Mississippi in search of a good location for their fur-trading company. The land that later became St. Louis was ideal. It had good access to the river and was protected from flooding by a natural hill on the riverbank. The location was also just 10 miles (16 kilometers) south of the Mississippi River's **confluence** with the Missouri River, the main **tributary** of the Mississippi. This location provided opportunities to trade along both the Missouri and the Mississippi rivers.

In 1764, Laclede and Chouteau returned to the location and founded St. Louis. They named it after the former King of France, Louis IX, who had become a saint in 1297. The early settlement had little more than wooden buildings and a small fur-trading community. Most of the early trade took place between the French and the Native Americans of the Missouri River.

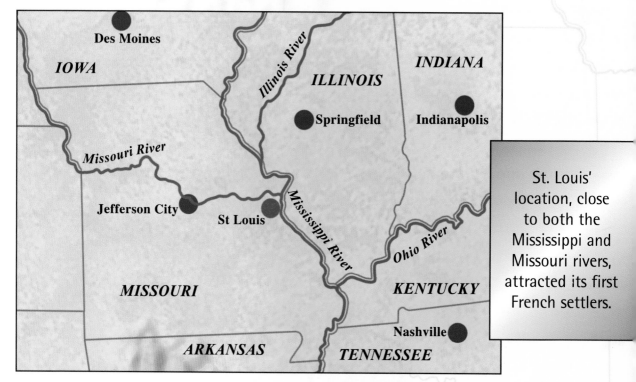

St. Louis' location, close to both the Mississippi and Missouri rivers, attracted its first French settlers.

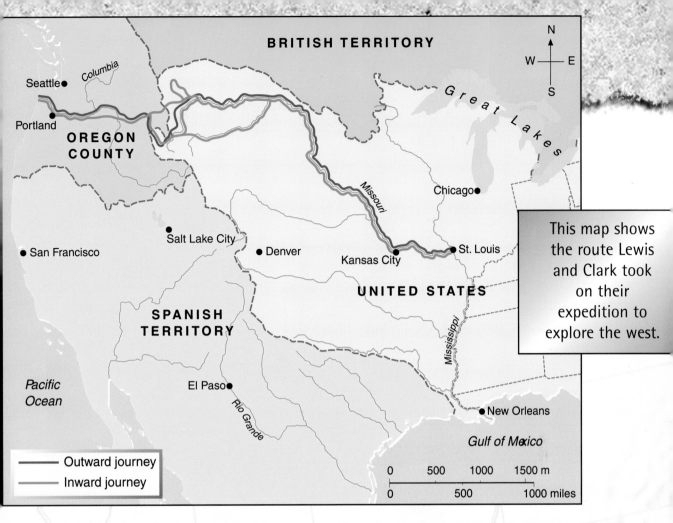

Seattle
Columbia
Portland
OREGON
COUNTY

Great Lakes

Chicago

Missouri

Salt Lake City
Denver
Kansas City
St. Louis

San Francisco

UNITED STATES

SPANISH
TERRITORY

Mississippi

Pacific
Ocean

El Paso

Rio Grande

New Orleans

Gulf of Mexico

Outward journey
Inward journey

0   500   1000   1500 m
0   500   1000 miles

This map shows the route Lewis and Clark took on their expedition to explore the west.

Early settlers relied on supplies brought by boat up the Mississippi, but soon St. Louis established itself as an important center for north–south trade along the Mississippi. By 1800, St. Louis had a busy waterfront and a permanent population of around a thousand people. It soon had boatmakers, general stores, and cargo warehouses. However, fur trading was still the most important part of St. Louis' **economy**.

Gateway to the west

After the **Louisiana Purchase** of 1803, St. Louis became part of the United States. The following year, President Thomas Jefferson sent Meriwether Lewis and William Clark to explore the new territories of the Louisiana Purchase. They chose St. Louis as the starting point for this famous exploration of the western United States that hadn't yet been explored by the Europeans and Americans. After gathering supplies in St. Louis, Lewis and Clark headed west along the Missouri River on May 14, 1804. They did not return to St. Louis until September 23, 1806. However, when they did, there was much celebration and excitement. They had opened the way for the exploration of the west. In addition, St. Louis became the starting point where settlers could gather supplies and equipment for their long journey west. This is why St. Louis became known as "the Gateway City."

25

The age of the steamboat

Steamboats arrived in St. Louis in 1817, and they had a huge influence on the city for the next 60 years. The riverfront in St. Louis was changed to allow the new steamboats to dock. Dirt **levees** were replaced with stone **wharves,** and warehouses were built to handle the increase in goods being transported by river. In 1849, St. Louis suffered a setback when a steamer exploded and started a fire. Because most of St. Louis' buildings were made of timber, the fire spread very quickly and destroyed a large part of the city.

St. Louis was rebuilt with stone and iron. The river played an important role in the rebuilding. Steamboats brought iron ore upstream from mines around 60 miles (100 kilometers) south of St. Louis. The river trade also provided money for the rebuilding effort. By the mid-1850s, the city was thriving again. Steamboats were sometimes lined three-deep along the city's riverfront, and St. Louis became one of the most important U.S. ports.
At the start of the Civil War in 1861, the use of iron became

Many of St. Louis' buildings, which were made of wood, were destroyed in a fire in 1849.

Mississippi earthquakes

On February 7, 1812, St. Louis was rocked by one of several earthquakes that occurred in the Mississippi valley at that time. The earthquake was one of the biggest in U.S. history. The force of the earthquake flattened several houses and damaged many others. In some places, the Mississippi changed its course. Small boats were destroyed or washed onto dry land. In other areas, riverbanks collapsed into the water and caused local flooding. Witnesses even reported that for a short time the river flowed backward! Thankfully, only one person was killed in the earthquake. Today, a similar earthquake would cost many lives and would cause billions of dollars of damage.

especially important. A St. Louis businessman named James Eads realized that control of the Mississippi and its trade would help shape the outcome of the war. He convinced the government to make a fleet of iron-clad steamboats to defend the river. These became known as the iron ships of St. Louis. They played a major part in helping Union forces capture and defend several Mississippi settlements. After the war, Eads went on to build the first railroad bridge across the Mississippi at St. Louis.

Eads Bridge in St. Louis was opened in 1874. It was the world's first steel-truss span and is still in use today. It is a national historic landmark.

Decline and revival

When the railroad arrived, it changed the fortunes of St. Louis. It gave the city major transportation connections in all directions. The river could handle goods traveling north and south while the new railroad connection across the Mississippi allowed goods to travel east and west. In the 1880s, the use of steamboats began to lessen. The railroad network grew rapidly, and this dramatically changed transportation in the United States. By the 1920s, the railroad had replaced much of the river trade. However, river transportation began to recover when **towboats** and **barges** replaced the steamers. During the 1900s, the port at St. Louis expanded into a giant complex.

In 1904 St. Louis held a world's fair to celebrate the 100th anniversary of the Louisiana Purchase. More than 20 million people visited St. Louis from over 40 countries. It is the biggest event ever recorded in the history of St. Louis.

1763	1803	1804
Pierre Laclede and August Chouteau discover the site that becomes St. Louis.	St. Louis becomes part of the USA.	Expedition to explore the western U.S. sets off from St. Louis.

Today the port of St. Louis stretches 70 miles (115 kilometers) along both sides of the Mississippi. There are 134 piers, wharves, docks wand 55 fleeting areas (where fleets of barges can tie up while waiting for towboats). The main cargoes passing through the port of St. Louis today are **petroleum,** chemicals, coal, and grain.

The population of the city and its suburbs is now around 2.1 million. In the second half of the 1900s, the city-center riverfront was redeveloped. One of the greatest achievements was the Gateway Arch, a steel arch standing 630 feet (192 meters) high that reminds visitors about the pioneers who set out from this historic gateway to the west.

Revolutions in transport

During the early 1900s, St. Louis became a center of car and aircraft manufacturing. The car industry developed from the wagons built in St. Louis for the pioneers. Between 1900 and 1930, over 200 car manufacturers operated in the city. Today, St. Louis is still a major car manufacturer.

Charles Lindberg became the first person to fly non-stop across the Atlantic Ocean in 1927. St. Louis businesses sponsored him, and he named his plane The Spirit of St. Louis. *In 1939 James McDonnell built a factory to make fighter aircraft for World War II. It later became part of Boeing, the world's largest manufacturer of commercial aircraft.*

1817	1849	1874	1920s
First steamboat arrives in St. Louis.	A steamer explodes and causes a large fire in St. Louis.	Eads Bridge opens in St. Louis.	Railroad replaces much of the river trade in St. Louis.

Memphis: Cotton and Music

A Native American stronghold

The first European to see the site that became Memphis was
Hernando de Soto in 1541. The land around Memphis was at
this time controlled by the Chickasaw people, who lived among
the forested river **bluffs** of the Mississippi. The Chicasaw hunted
bison, deer, and bears in the forest. They caught fish from the
Mississippi. The Chicasaw also grew crops such as corn, beans,
and squash.

In the 1700s, the French, Spanish, British, and later
the Americans competed for control of the Mississippi River.
During this period, different forts were built at what was
to become Memphis to protect river trade along the Mississippi.
The city itself was not founded until the following century.

FACT

One of Memphis's founders, Andrew
Jackson, went on to become the
seventh president of the United States
(1829 to 1837).

Memphis was founded in 1819.
The Mississippi provided an
important trading
route and also made the area's
soil fertile.

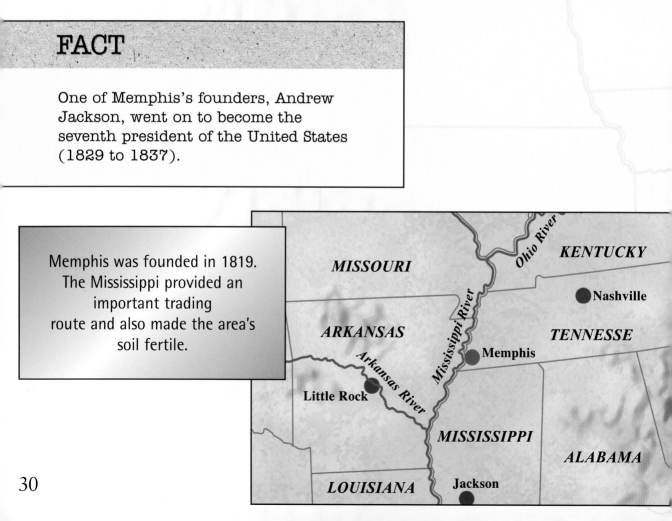

In 1818, the Chickasaw passed their lands to the United States. Memphis was founded the following year on May 22, by John Overton, James Winchester, and Andrew Jackson.

Workers pick cotton in the plantations that grew up around Memphis and along the Mississippi River.

King Cotton

From its very beginnings, Memphis was an important market town and trading post. This was due to its location on one of the busiest trade routes in the country between St. Louis (upstream) and New Orleans (downstream). German and Irish **immigrants** built many of the early businesses and some of the city's oldest buildings. Memphis became more important thanks to cotton, which was sometimes called "white gold." The countryside around Memphis was ideal for growing cotton because it had very rich soils. These fertile soils had been deposited over thousands of years by the flooding Mississippi. As the waters receded, they left behind soils rich in **minerals** and nutrients. The climate around Memphis, which included warm summers and plenty of rain, was also suited to cotton.

For the cotton industry, Memphis's greatest feature was its location on the Mississippi River. This made it easy to transport cotton to Europe and the more industrialized northern states. The **steamboat** was the main means of transportation at this time. Memphis soon developed a busy waterfront. By the middle of the 1800s, Memphis had become the cotton capital of the mid-south. In fact, it was so famous as a cotton center that it became known as "King Cotton."

31

City of slaves

Memphis owed much of its early growth and prosperity to slavery. Thousands of slaves were brought to the city to work on cotton plantations, which required many workers. Most of the slaves came from West African countries where they were captured and sold to slave dealers. The slaves were then shipped across the Atlantic Ocean and up the Mississippi River to be sold to plantation owners as cotton pickers or house slaves. Conditions for the slaves were extremely hard, and many did not even survive the crossing. Those that did were bought and sold in auctions, like cattle at a livestock sale.

Memphis was not affected much during the **Civil War,** and it continued to grow. However, during one river battle in June 1862 the iron-clad gunboats of the Union fleet took Memphis from the Confederates. It is said that 10,000 people lined the hills along the Mississippi to watch the battle for Memphis. The end of the Civil War also marked the end of slavery in the United States. Many former slaves settled in Memphis, and they quickly developed a strong black community with their own churches and neighborhoods.

A market in Memphis sells slaves as workers for the cotton plantations.

A Memphis resident named Ed Shaw became one of the most powerful African Americans of the time. He served on the city council and was also elected **wharf** master of the riverfront. Because of the importance of the river, this was an important and well-paid job.

Memphis' history as a slave center has been part of its culture ever since. The songs and rhythms that African slaves brought with them to Memphis led to a new form of music known as the blues, which developed from the 1890s onward. Memphis was one of the most important cities for early blues music. Many of the first blues musicians played in the city, particularly on world-famous Beale Street. The Mississippi River has inspired many blues musicians to write songs about the river and the people who live and work on it. One

of the most famous songs is *Mississippi Delta Blues*, which was written by W. C. Handy. Handy also wrote the songs *Memphis Blues* and *St. Louis' Blues*.

Birthplace of rock and roll

Not only is Memphis famous as the home of the blues, it is also considered to be the birthplace of rock and roll. Memphis is especially associated with Elvis Presley, who was influenced by blues music and lived and died in the city. Presley was one of the most influential musicians of all time. His home, Graceland, in Memphis, is now a museum dedicated to his life. Except from the White House in Washington, Graceland is the most visited house in the United States.

Trade and tourism

Throughout the 1900s, the Mississippi River continued to be important in the development of Memphis. Cotton was still star of the **economy.** By the mid-1900s the city traded more than 40 percent of all cotton produced in the United States. Other important **commodities** traded in Memphis include timber, grain, **petroleum,** coal, and manufactured goods. New port facilities were built in 1946 on President's Island just downstream of the central business district to handle the growing amount of river traffic. At one time, President's Island was the biggest island in the Mississippi. However, it has been connected to the mainland to protect one side of it from the risk of flooding. This sheltered side is where the new port facilities have been built.

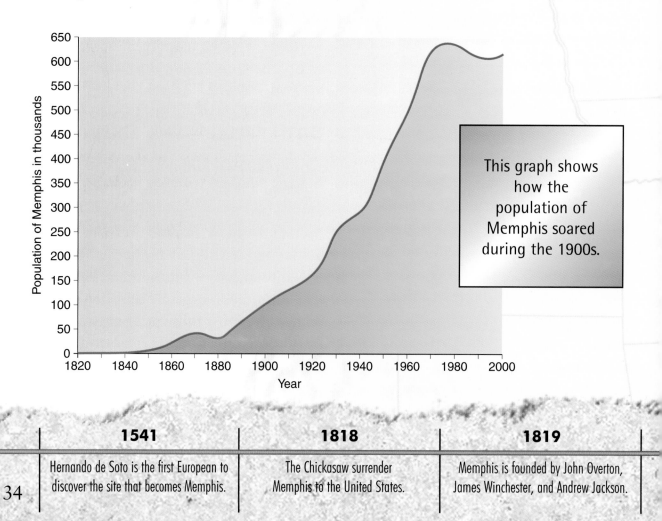

This graph shows how the population of Memphis soared during the 1900s.

1541	1818	1819
Hernando de Soto is the first European to discover the site that becomes Memphis.	The Chickasaw surrender Memphis to the United States.	Memphis is founded by John Overton, James Winchester, and Andrew Jackson.

The port of Memphis is now one of the United States' chief transportation and distribution centers. Each year, about 30,000 railroad cars pass through the port. The port also has connections to Memphis International Airport, which is the world's biggest cargo airport.

In the 1980s, city officials began redeveloping Memphis waterfront to attract more tourists. One of the city's newest attractions was a 32-story pyramid, which was built on the banks of the Mississippi in 1991. This unusual building is a sports and entertainment arena, but it has become a popular city attraction in its own right. In May each year, the Mississippi becomes the focus of a music and cultural festival called Memphis in May. Many of the festival events take place in Tom Lee Park, which is located along the river.

The park is named after a **levee** worker who became a hero after he rescued 32 people from a sinking river steamer in 1925.

One of Memphis' biggest tourist attractions is Mud Island River Park. The island park is home to the Mississippi River Museum, where visitors can learn about the natural and cultural history of the river. Mud Island River Park shows that although Memphis might be changing, the river is still central to the city, its economy, and its people.

FACT

Memphis' Pyramid Arena is taller than the Statue of Liberty in New York and the Taj Mahal in India.

1946	1980s	1991
New port facilities are built in Memphis.	Redevelopment of Memphis' city center and waterfront.	32-storey pyramid built in Memphis.

Minneapolis: The Milling Capital

Sacred falls

The city of Minneapolis lies at the **confluence** of the
Mississippi and Minnesota rivers. It has a twin city,
St. Paul, located a little further to the south. Minneapolis is
located on land that once belonged to the Dakota people.
This meeting of the rivers was considered by the Dakota to be
the spiritual center of their world. Especially important were
a set of waterfalls on the Mississippi. The Dakota called them
Owamniyomni, which means "the whirlpool." They are in
fact the only natural waterfalls on the entire Mississippi
River. The first European to see them was a Belgian priest
named Louis Hennepin. He visited the area during the early
1680s and gave them the name St. Anthony's Falls after his
favorite saint.

The falls were to play an important role in the development
of Minneapolis. However, it was over 200 years before any
form of permanent **settlement** was established on the site. In
1805, the Dakota surrendered the land that became
Minneapolis to the growing power of the United States. In

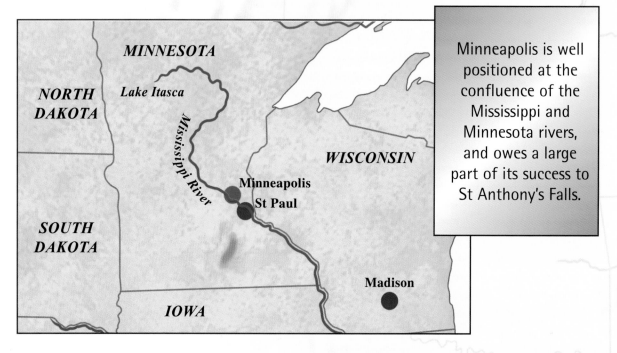

Minneapolis is well
positioned at the
confluence of the
Mississippi and
Minnesota rivers,
and owes a large
part of its success to
St Anthony's Falls.

SEPT 16-1901

A view of Minneapolis in 1901. These logs are being sorted at Boom Island.

1819, the Americans built a fort at the confluence of the Mississippi and Minnesota rivers to control the surrounding lands. The need for timber to build the fort led to the construction of saw **mills** at St. Anthony's Falls. The force of the falling water provided energy to power the mills. Logs were brought down by river from forests upstream. Flour mills were also built at the falls to help feed soldiers at the fort. Both industries used the power of the Mississippi River and led to the founding of Minneapolis.

The first settlement was the small village of St. Anthony. It was located on the eastern side of the Mississippi across from the present-day city of Minneapolis. Settlers arrived there in the late 1840s, and the settlement became a city in 1855. Also that year, the city was linked to Minneapolis by a suspension bridge that spanned the river. Minneapolis itself was first settled and named in 1852. The name comes from the Dakota word *minnehaha*, which means "laughing waters," and *polis*, which is Greek for "city." The idea for the name came from a schoolteacher, who wrote to the local paper with the proposed name. It was widely welcomed and quickly adopted. In 1872, the settlement of St. Anthony became part of Minneapolis. Old St. Anthony is still a neighborhood of the city today.

Milling capital of the world

Minneapolis soon began to prosper, thanks to its special position along St. Anthony's Falls. The water was taken from above the falls by a system of canals. The energy of the falling water was used to turn waterwheels and to generate power, then the water was returned to the river downstream of the falls. Minneapolis grew rapidly as sawmills and flour mills were built to take advantage of the falls' power. The river also provided the transportation route for bringing raw materials (grain and logs) in and for sending finished goods (flour and timber) out.

By 1880, Minneapolis had become the flour-milling capital of the world. It held on to this title for 50 years. The Washburn "A" Mill was a special success, even though it suffered a huge explosion shortly after it was built in 1874. It was the most technologically advanced mill in the world, and at its peak could grind enough flour in a single day to bake 12 million loaves of bread! Timber production also reached its height around this time. By 1889, Minneapolis was America's leading sawmill center.

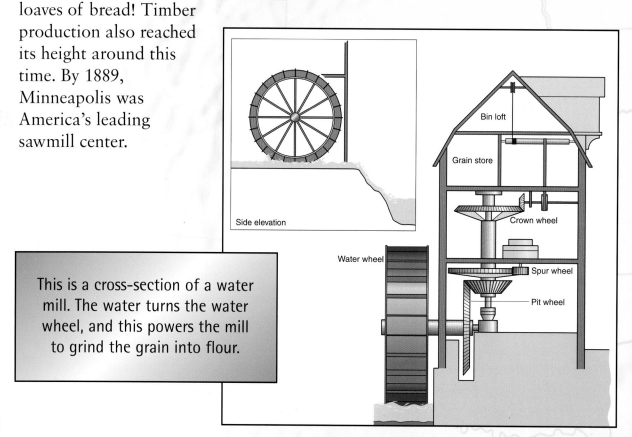

Side elevation

Bin loft

Grain store

Crown wheel

Water wheel

Spur wheel

Pit wheel

This is a cross-section of a water mill. The water turns the water wheel, and this powers the mill to grind the grain into flour.

By 1890, the population of Minneapolis had grown from around 13,000 in 1870 to 165,000. Most of the people were laborers who came to work in the mills or industries connected to them. Toward the end of the 1800s, the railroads boosted the growth of Minneapolis. Huge farms in the northwest were planted with wheat, and their harvests were transported into Minneapolis by hundreds of rail wagons.

The timber industry still depended on the Mississippi for bringing logs down to Minneapolis from the forests of the north. In 1899, so many logs were transported in this way that they completely blocked the river above Minneapolis. By 1906, the forests of the north had been cleared, and Minneapolis's sawmills were in decline. The last sawmill closed in 1921, but the flour mills continued until well into the 1960s.

Minneapolis was at the center of the U.S. grain and flour industry, and it became a major financial market as well as a manufacturing center. The Minneapolis Grain Exchange was founded in 1881. It rapidly became the United States' most important grain market. Banking and insurance soon followed to meet the demands of farmers, millers, and other customers. These financial industries gradually took over during the 1900s. Today they are the main **economic** activity in Minneapolis.

This 1949 photo shows the Pillsbury "A" Mill in Minneapolis, one of the biggest mills on the river.

FACT

So much water was taken from the Mississippi to power the mills of Minneapolis that St. Anthony's Falls were sometimes known to dry up.

Stairway of water

The only waterfalls on the Mississippi, St. Anthony's Falls created a break in the **navigation** of the Mississippi River. They prevented steamboats from traveling beyond St. Paul, the twin city of Minneapolis located just downstream. From there, people and goods had to transfer to land for the onward journey. The first plans to extend navigation above the falls were set down in 1850, but it would be more than 100 years before these plans were achieved. Early attempts to control the flow of St. Anthony's Falls had ended in disaster and destroyed large sections of the waterfall. It was not until 1885 that the U.S. Army Corps of Engineers finally stabilized the falls.

Locks

A lock is an instrument used on rivers or canals that allows boats to be raised or lowered from one water level to another. The main feature of a lock is a chamber with gates that can be opened and closed at either end. The water in the chamber is controlled by opening or shutting paddles. Once the boat reaches the correct level, the gates are opened and the boat continues its journey either upstream or downstream.

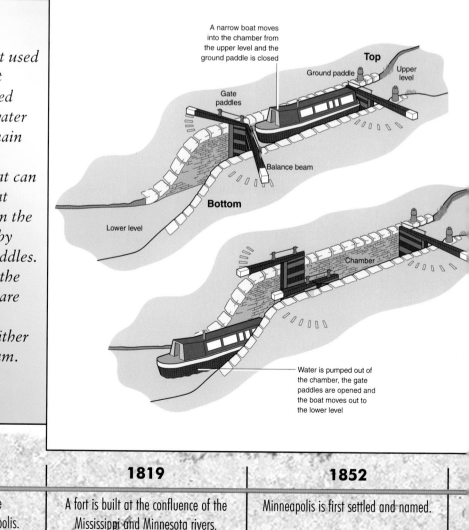

A narrow boat moves into the chamber from the upper level and the ground paddle is closed

Top

Ground paddle

Upper level

Gate paddles

Balance beam

Bottom

Lower level

Chamber

Water is pumped out of the chamber, the gate paddles are opened and the boat moves out to the lower level

1680	1819	1852
Louis Hennepin names the St. Anthony's Falls at Minneapolis.	A fort is built at the confluence of the Mississippi and Minnesota rivers.	Minneapolis is first settled and named.

A photo from 1954 of a ship lock being built alongside St Anthony's Falls in Minneapolis. The locks have greatly boosted river cargo on the Mississippi.

In the first half of the 1900s, navigation between Minneapolis and St. Louis was improved when a series of locks and dams were built along the Mississippi. St. Anthony's Falls still presented a natural barrier. This was finally overcome in 1963, when two new locks were completed to guide river traffic above Minneapolis for the first time.

Today the locks over St. Anthony's Falls are vital to the navigation of the upper Mississippi. Before they were completed, **barge** traffic on the upper Mississippi River handled around 27 million tons of cargo each year. This has now increased to around 80 million tons a year.

The locks also make it possible for pleasure boats to navigate the river, and they have even become a popular tourist attraction in their own right. Together with its twin city of St. Paul, Minneapolis is now home to around 2.5 million people. They all owe their success in some way to the Mississippi. In September 2003, a new museum, The Mill City Museum, opened in Minneapolis to celebrate this fact. It acts as a reminder to future generations of the time when Minneapolis was the world's greatest mill town.

1855	1872	1881	1963
St. Anthony becomes a city and is connected to Minneapolis by a suspension bridge.	St. Anthony becomes part of Minneapolis.	Minneapolis Grain Exchange founded.	Two new locks guide river traffic above Minneapolis for the first time.

The Mississippi of Tomorrow

What does the future hold?

The Mississippi River of today would be barely recognizable to the explorers and pioneers who founded its early **settlements.** Cities such as St. Louis and New Orleans, which were once small trading villages, are now vast cities with millions of people. One thing they would recognize, however, is the importance of the river as a major trade route. Although the type of transportation and cargo seen on the Mississippi might have changed, the river is still a vital waterway for the people and settlements living along it. But what will the future hold for the Mississippi and its settlements?

Tourism is almost certain to increase. Memphis and New Orleans are already especially popular tourist destinations. However, all of the Mississippi's settlements are likely to receive more tourists. One feature that will increase tourism, and bring all the settlements of the Mississippi closer together is the Mississippi River Trail.

FACT

In 2000, the Mississippi River handled 30 percent of all U.S. water-borne trade.

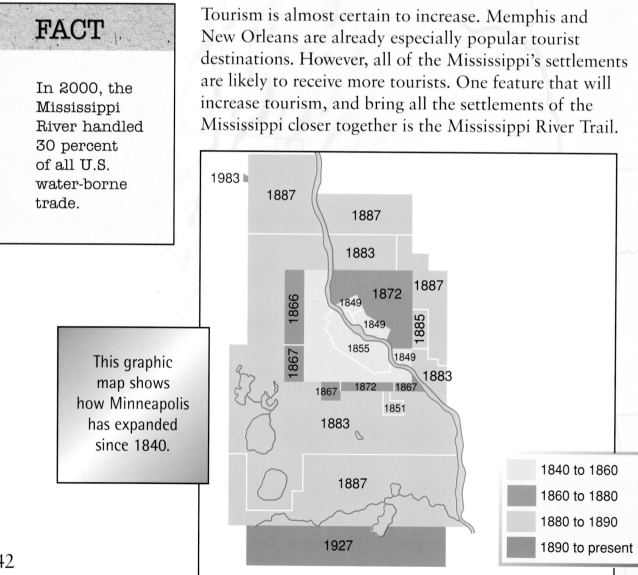

This graphic map shows how Minneapolis has expanded since 1840.

1983
1887
1887
1883
1887
1866
1849
1872
1849
1885
1855
1849
1867
1883
1867
1872
1867
1851
1883
1887
1927

	1840 to 1860
	1860 to 1880
	1880 to 1890
	1890 to present

These tourists are on board a modern **steamboat** on the Mississippi River.

This will be a 2,000-mile (3,220-kilometer) bicycle trail that follows the Mississippi through ten states. Parts of the trail are already open, but others will be added soon. The river itself remains a major tourist attraction for river cruises or other boating activities on the Mississippi.

Living with the Mississippi

For as long as people have lived along the Mississippi, they have had to cope with the risk of flooding. This continues to be true. The last major flood on the Mississippi took place in 1993. It covered land in 9 states, damaged about 56,000 homes, and killed 50 people. St. Louis was under great threat during the floods, but the **levee** walls held back the waters and protected the city and its people. In

rural areas, many of the levees did not hold, and others were too low. After the flood, thousands of miles of levees along the Mississippi and its **tributaries were in need of repair.**

The 1993 floods led to great debates about the future of the Mississippi River. Some believe that antiflood measures, such as levee construction to protect settlements and farmland, might have contributed to the flooding. Others argue that without the levees, the damage would have been much greater. For example, they say that St. Louis would have been badly flooded, causing billions of dollars of damage. In reality, a river as mighty as the Mississippi is never likely to be tamed by the people living alongside it. Instead, the people have to learn to live with the river—and its floods.

43

Timeline

6000 B.C.E.	Native Americans live along the Mississippi River.
1541 C.E.	Hernando de Soto discovers the Mississippi.
1682	French explorers discover the site that becomes New Orleans.
1718	Jean-Baptiste le Moyne de Bienville plans New Orleans.
1719	Fort is built by the French at Baton Rouge.
1763	France gives New Orleans to the Spanish.
1763	Pierre Laclede and August Chouteau discover the site that becomes St. Louis.
1789	United States of America is founded.
1803	United States buys New Orleans in the **Louisiana Purchase.**
1803	St Louis becomes part of the United States.
1804	Expedition to explore the west sets off from St. Louis.
1811–1812	Several severe earthquakes occur in the Mississippi valley.
1812	First **steamboat** arrives in Baton Rouge.
1817	First steamboat arrives in St. Louis.
1818	The Chickasaw surrender Memphis to the United States.
1819	Memphis is founded by John Overton, James Winchester, and Andrew Jackson.
1819	Pentagon Barracks are built at Baton Rouge.
1832	Itasca Lake is named by explorer Henry Rowe Schoolcraft.
1849	A steamer explodes and causes a large fire in St. Louis.
1862	Union forces claim Baton Rouge and slaves are freed.
1862	Battle over Memphis in the **Civil War.**
1874	Eads Bridge opens in St. Louis.
1883	Railroad arrives in Baton Rouge.
1885	U.S. Army Corps of Engineers stabilize St. Anthony's Falls.
1890s	Blues music develops in Memphis.
1900s	Jazz music begins to develop in New Orleans.
1909	Standard Oil build a new refinery in Baton Rouge.
1920s	Railroad replaces much of the river trade in St. Louis.
1921	Last sawmill closes in Minneapolis.
1946	New port facilities are built in Memphis.
1980s	Redevelopment of Memphis city center and waterfront.
1991	32-story pyramid is built in Memphis.
2003	Mill City Museum opens in Minneapolis.

Further Resources

Books

Currie, Stephen. *Rivers of the World: The Mississippi*. Lucent Books, 2002.

Curtis, Martin and Milligan, Simon. *A River Journey: The Mississippi*. Hodder Wayland, 2003.

Pollard. Michael. *The Mississippi*. Evans Brothers, 1997.

Using the Internet

Where to search
A search engine will look through the entire web and list all the sites that match the words in the search box. Try **www.google.com**. A search directory is a library of websites that have been sorted by a person instead of a computer. You can search by keyword or subject and browse through different related sites. A good example is **yahooligans.com**.

Search tips
There are billions of pages on the Internet, so it can be difficult to find exactly what you want. These search skills will help you find useful websites more quickly:
- Use two to six simple keywords, putting the most important words first.
- Be precise, only use names of people, places or things.
- If you want to find words that go together, put quotation marks around them, for example "St Anthony's falls" or "Gateway Arch".
- Going to the "cached" option of a result will highlight where the keywords you searched for appear on the website.

Glossary

altitude height above sea level, measured in feet or meters

archaeology study of the past using evidence that was left behind, usually found buried underground

barge narrow, long, flat-bottomed boat used for carrying goods. Some barges also carry people.

bayou area of slow-moving water. A bayou is often swampy and overgrown with water-loving plants.

bluff a steep hill, mound, or cliff

Civil War war fought in the United States from 1861 to 1865 between the Confederates and the Unionists

commodity item that is bought and sold. This term is usually used to describe raw materials and farm produce.

confluence point where two (or more) river channels meet

delta area at the mouth of a river, formed by the deposit of sand and soil in a triangular shape

economy goods and services produced and used by a community

flatboat wooden boat with a flat bottom that is directed down a river using long poles. It was common on the Mississippi River before the arrival of the steamboat in the early 1800s.

floodplain land to the side of a river that is frequently flooded during periods when the river is in full flow

immigrant person who moves into an area from somewhere outside (often another country)

irrigation watering crops using specially created systems, normally used in areas of low rainfall

levee artificial embankment built alongside a river channel to protect land from being flooded

Louisiana Purchase the sale of a large part of modern-day western United States by France to the newly formed U.S. government in 1803

lumber wood taken from trees that has been sawed and prepared for use in building or manufacturing

Mardi Gras alternative name for Shrove Tuesday. In New Orleans this is celebrated with a major street carnival involving musicians, dancing, and brightly colored costumes.

meander wind from side to side rather than follow a direct (straight) route

metropolitan city and its surrounding suburbs

mill building that houses machinery used to convert raw materials into finished goods, such as grain into flour, or timber into lumber

mineral substance found naturally in the ground and mined for its value. Coal, gold, and iron ore are minerals.

molasses syrup produced by the processing and manufacture of raw sugar

navigable possible to travel by ship or boat

navigation act of directing or moving a boat along a river or across a lake or sea

petrochemical substance made from petroleum or natural gas, such as gasoline, paraffin, or kerosene

petroleum crude oil that is used to make a variety of petrochemicals, such as gasoline and kerosene fuels

reaches part of a river's course. Rivers are normally divided into middle, upper, and lower reaches.

settlement place that has people permanently living in it. Settlements can vary in size from a small village to a large city.

shrine place of worship, normally linked to a holy site or a holy person

silt soil and gravel carried by a river and deposited as it slows down, along its banks, its bottom, or in its delta

steamboat (or steamer) boat in which the engine is powered by the production of steam, usually by burning coal

territory of Louisiana area of the United States and Canada that was once under the control of the French. It included, but was much bigger than, the present-day state of Louisiana.

textile manufactured cloth or fabric, made by weaving or knitting

towboat a powerful boat used to tow or push cargo barges along a river. One towboat may be able to move fifteen large barges.

tributary river or stream that joins another, normally larger, river

wharf structure built alongside, or into, a river channel that enables boats to dock and unload their goods or passengers

Index